SWEET SPOT
LEADERSHIP

Derek,
You'r Awsome!.
Scott

SCOTT SIMONS

ISBN: 1491024003
ISBN 13: 9781491024003
Library of Congress Control Number: 2013913085
CreateSpace Independent Publishing Platform
North Charleston, South Carolina

Dedication

This book is dedicated to a great man who learned leadership at a young age while serving his country in World War II. His ability to learn quickly and to lead by example gave him the skills to be very focused. He always reinforced the importance of self-reliance and that has guided my sister and me on our paths in life. Today, more than ever, his generation deserves the name that was coined, "the Greatest," as their legacy lives on.

I was proud to call this great man Dad… He always knew where the Sweetest Spots of all came from and that was his family. The light shined on my mom and his grandchildren Jocelyn and Dylan.

To the loving memory of Robert Simons, (Big Bob).

Table of Contents

Acknowledgements

This book sits squarely on the shoulders of the many mentors that have given me the knowledge, friendship, and clarity that have served me well as I continue onwards. Many of these individuals had no idea that their day-to-day input and sage advice would fuel my desire to continue my quest to always be learning and to never take anything for granted. These mentors whose numbers are too great to name know who they are as I thank them as often as I can.

Preface

Is it time to find the sweet spot that creates value? Is it time to show the world what you and your business really have to offer?

If so, this book will help you stop being the best-kept secret in your industry, niche or region – and reveal your products, services, and value as the "secret sauce" that is essential to your prospects' and customers' success.

As a business owner, you may feel that you have been commoditized, compromised, and just plain used.

It does not have to be that way.

Time and daily pressures diminish your natural appetite for innovation. If you are like most business owners I work with, you often do not make the proactive changes necessary to fully maximize the value in your business.

At the same time, most business owners think they know their business better than anyone else (and certainly better than any business book author!).

That "my way or the highway" thinking has left much potential value, revenue, and profit on the table.

No matter what industry you are in, and no matter how long you have been in business, there is more value that you can deliver for your clients, customers, prospects, employees, vendors, partners, suppliers, franchisees and yourself than you think.

This short book will show you where to find the sweet spot and create the value in your business to create the lasting success you deserve.

Using the interactive exercises and tools, you can also use this as a *field guide* to find value and to change the way your business operates, serves customers, and serves *you, the owner.*

The guide to find the sweet spot is now in your hands. Please use it wisely.

Section I –
Transformative Leaders

From Entrepreneur to Leader

Steve Jobs, the late CEO of Apple, is well known for his incredible innovations and success. But surprisingly, he attributed much of that wild success to something most would consider a terrible failure; in 1985 he was fired from Apple, the company he helped to create.

In the commencement address Jobs gave to Stanford University in 2005, he said, "I didn't see it then, but it turned out that getting fired from Apple was the best thing that could have ever happened to me. The heaviness of being successful was replaced by the lightness of being a beginner again, less sure about everything. It freed me to enter into one of the most creative periods of my life."

Part of what made Jobs such an incredible leader was how he used this setback as an opportunity to learn. He was able to use that failure as a transformative moment and in so doing became a transformative leader. When he returned as the CEO of Apple years later, he did so as a true businessman who would lead the company to develop products that would change entire industries.

In the same address to Stanford, he concluded, "I'm pretty sure none of this would have happened if I hadn't been fired from Apple. It was awful tasting medicine, but I guess the patient needed it. Sometimes life hits you in the head with a brick. Don't lose faith. I'm convinced the only thing that kept me going was that I loved what I did. You've got to find what you love."

What Is Transformative Leadership?

Are you an entrepreneur who has dreamed of building a company that has real value? Are you hoping your great idea will automatically translate into growth and success?

As many entrepreneurs before you have learned, it is necessary to have more than just an excellent product or service. Many who start out with great ideas fail to take their company to the next level.

To truly be a leader and build the type of company you want, you must become a *transformative* leader. You must be willing to make changes. You also need to be prepared to guide your company as you transform to capitalize on opportunities that will help you to grow.

So what must you do to be a transformative leader? Not everyone will have a clear Steve Jobs moment of drastic change to signal a shift. If you make the decision to transform, you don't need any outside factors to push you.

Transformative leaders educate themselves. Reading this book is an excellent start, but you should be looking to many sources of information to build your knowledge base. Speak with investment bankers, industry leaders, your customers— you need to learn as much as possible to guide your leadership.

Transformative leaders identify the areas that require change and develop new processes to improve them. Take a hard look at how your company is conducting business. Don't just continue operating under the status quo. Identify what is not working and find a solution that will yield better results.

Transformative leaders reflect and evaluate their businesses on a continuing basis. The initial evaluation is extremely important, but just as important is monitoring the company regularly to understand the impact of your changes. Transformative leaders need to be able to continue transforming to reach the best result.

Transformative leaders know that change is hard but the transformation is going to be worth it. There will certainly be some growing pains as you make these necessary changes. You will likely encounter pushback from your employees who are resistant to the unfamiliar. You need to be prepared to guide them through it and be a champion for the growth you hope to achieve.

Transformative leaders find the sweet spot. You need to identify the unique "sweet spot" for your company that creates real value. This will be the focus of your growth and will be a key element of your transformative leadership.

What Is Your Sweet Spot?

Most people think the phrase "sweet spot" comes from the world of sports. According to William Safire of *The New York Times*, the sweet spot is the place somewhere on the thickest part of the bat that the batter believes gives him the most power and control.

In his 2007 essay Safire said golfers may lay claim to the phrase's origin. "Trigonometry Finds 'Sweet Spot' for the Golf Club to Meet the Ball" was a headline in *The New York Times* of March 16, 1957. It is the place on the ball, just below the center of the sphere, that – when hit squarely to generate the proper amount of backspin – leads to the longest drive.

Actually, the earliest reference comes not from sports or business, but from literature. In the "Council of War" chapter of Robert Louis Stevenson's 1883 *Treasure Island*, Long John Silver, the dread peg-leg pirate, tells the narrator, "Ah . . . this here is a sweet spot, this island – a sweet spot for a lad to get ashore on. You'll bathe, and you'll climb trees, and you'll hunt goats. . . . Why, it makes me young again."

In business the phrase is a more exhilarating version of the happy medium.

"Remember the tale of Goldilocks and the Three Bears?" wrote Safire. "She faced three bowls of the bears' cereal, tasted one and exclaimed, 'This porridge is too hot!' The next was too cold, but the third caused her to purr, 'Ahhh, this porridge is just right,' and 'she ate it all up,' to the consternation of the returning three bears. Economists wondering whether the economy is overheating or cooling hope we are in 'the Goldilocks economy' – just right – and those who are bearish or bullish today may soon wonder whatever happened to today's sweet spot."

The term is widely used today because it speaks to an aspiration of many. Joe Pickett, then executive editor of *The American Heritage Dictionary*, told Safire that sweet spots are proliferating in popular usage and "refer to an area of range surrounded by or lying between less favorable conditions."

This is the entrepreneurs' sweet spot quest: to create a profitable business that thrives in just the right range of creating value, while others struggle to survive in an environment of less favorable conditions.

Where's the Sweet Spot's Value?

In my experience as a CEO and business owner, I have seen many entrepreneurs seek to build a company that finds the sweet spot and creates real value.

So if this is the quest, why is it 8 out of 10 businesses fail within five years (according to a study by *Inc.* and the National Business Incubator Association) and the remainder sell for a fraction of what they could or should when it is time for the owner to move on?

Value is the essence of what determines a company's successes and failures. This term will be the guiding force of *Sweet Spot Leadership*; therefore, the concept of "value" needs a strong foundation.

To quote Thomas Edison, "The value of an idea lies in the using of it." A good idea is limited to just that: good. It takes execution and understanding to actually succeed on a higher level.

Value is not just the price of your product or the assets you possess.

Value is the experience and benefits that you can offer to others.

Your business does not operate in a bubble. The network connecting clients, customers, advertisers, investors, and everyone else you contact is constantly growing. It is necessary, as an entrepreneur, to show all of these people just how significant your product or service can be.

Almost certainly, no one buys into the idea of your company on goodwill alone. Even a strong set of goods, ideas, or assets is not convincing enough. Bringing the value is a more rounded and all-encompassing view of establishing a great business model. It comes from the right combination of price and quality, the right market presence, the right touch in planning for the future, and far more.

So where do you start the journey to find the sweet spot and create real value? In the following chapters I will discuss how you can identify it. Begin with the ingredients that make you special. This may require intense internal focus and reaching out to your customers and market.

I will discuss the four crucial areas that you will need to focus on to get that sweet spot just right: Profitability, Leveragability, Customer Resonance, and Marketability.

The final section of the book will look at the tools you need to grow the company. While you are the leader, you can't do this on your own. You need to build the right team and guide them through the changes you are implementing. You need to nurture the sweet spot so it makes it through the transformation with real value. We will look at the kinds of evaluations you can be doing to keep on track.

2

Find the Sweet Spot – What is Your Secret Sauce?

Sometimes a line from an old movie says it all. Remember when every burger joint had a secret sauce?

In the 1982 film *Fast Times at Ridgemont High*, teenage workers from various fast food restaurants reveal what goes into the "secret sauce" for their hamburgers. One says "ketchup and mayonnaise," and the other says "thousand island dressing."

The joke was there was nothing that special about secret sauce. But for an entrepreneur that wants to find the sweet spot, your secret sauce is no laughing matter.

Ordinary won't cut the mustard. Only extraordinary will do.

Business owners see their companies in one of two ways:

1. Groundbreaking: Completely innovative and forming a new niche market.

2. Version 2.0: A new twist on a tried-and-true field or industry, the "me-too" companies.

After all, entrepreneurs start in either a new market, like the technology gurus (Apple, PayPal, Facebook), or they start in what they think is a pre-existing lucrative market (retail, food, entertainment).

A Groundbreaking Company is a:

- Trendsetter
- Category creator
- Brand-name leader

Products like Xerox copiers and Kleenex tissues have entered the everyday language we speak when discussing those markets. When people think of Donald Trump and high-end real estate, they instantly think: "Self-promoter, billionaire, entrepreneur, and well-branded."

A Version 2.0 Company is:

- The everyday business
- The store you always use
- Easily replaceable
- Not memorable
- A "me-too" business

If you walked by one of these types of companies and it had changed its name, you would barely even notice. Banks, hotels, and supermarkets in particular have become Version 2.0 companies, constantly changing, but still offering more of the same.

Problems occur if and when they use the most common type of messaging in their industry to attract clients. In doing so, they become (at best) just another me-too of that industry.

A new product branded and priced similarly to an industry leader will consistently lose to the brand-name item. As the newcomer, you need to assess where you want to take a stand.

A big mistake Version 2.0 companies make when entering new markets is to fail to see the niche that they should be serving. Instead they try to serve everyone; which results in serving no one well.

Jumping into a Market

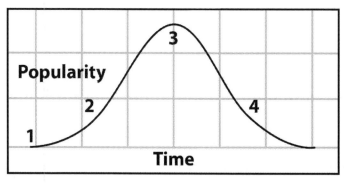

Take a look at the graph above. It displays the rise and fall of a good idea. Every new thought has a

Goldilocks effect – the point where it is "just right" to enter the market.

Jumping into a venture at point 1 makes you a Creator: the founder of a new and unknown idea.

By point 3, the market is saturated and the product is an industry standard. At point 4, the "next big thing" has already taken hold and your idea grows stale.

Point 2 (in conjunction with point 1) can both get you in the game, but 2 is certainly the perfect porridge – just right. People and businesses that operate at point 2 are known as Early Adopters and the early bird catches the worm.

Real value creators know their niche and spread their message only in that market. They drill deeper and deeper to become the go-to company in that industry.

My Story

My career began as an optician. I founded my first company, Simons Optical, at the age of 21. I went on to build several multi-million dollar enterprises. During the time I built these companies, I worked closely with private investment bankers and learned the inner workings of corporate America through exposure to companies like IBM and GE.

Today, I work closely with developing business owners, helping them to clearly see what to do with their companies. What I have seen time and time again in CEO Council meetings, and with the business owners that I work with individually, is that most businesses grow to a certain level and then fail to deliver on or communicate the full value that they are capable of offering to their clients.

Many have that nagging feeling that they do not have a secret sauce. They might kid themselves that they do not need one because it is pure hard work. If they get an occasional jolt of fear, they shrug it off and are comforted by the success they have had to date.

Value and Cost

Value creators are frequently also category creators. Starting outside of Philadelphia, entrepreneur David Schlessinger began the Five Below enterprise. As the name indicates, all products were five dollars or less. Five Below offered a higher quality and ostensibly more reliable line of goods than his competitors, but was not operating as "just another dollar store." Schlessinger opted to make his own opportunity.

But without that secret sauce, the company enters into the "treadmill period" where the business goes through the motions of doing the same thing, day after day, year after year—sometimes for more than fifteen or twenty years. As the owners watch revenue stagnate, the value that once was in the company gradually fades away.

The Simons Cycle

The Simons Cycle is a visualization of a fatigue that can hit a business of any size. If you, the entrepreneur, cannot find value at this critical juncture, then the business will swiftly deteriorate.

Value

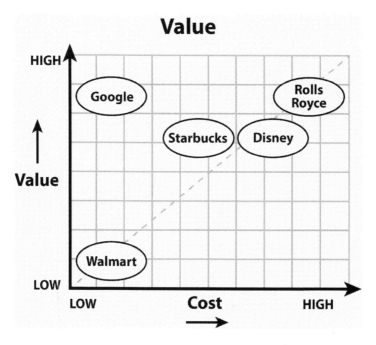

There is also a Sweet Spot when assessing value and cost. A product with high cost but low value will be perceived as a weak product. Unless it is the only one of its type (a monopoly or irreplaceable technology), this will fail. Conversely, a product with high value but low cost will not generate enough profit to be sustainable. An exception to this rule is Google, which has such a wide variety of services that it is self-sustaining.

The ideal is, again, a Goldilocks Effect: not too expensive, but a quality offering.

Price Pressure Syndrome

As your industry matures, your company has to increase the value of your offerings or risk the Price Pressure Syndrome that creeps into a mature industry. Price lowering is a surefire way to wipe out all the value in your business—and it happens in the blink of an eye.

Stagnation must be countered by innovation; however, there are practices or traps that can hinder a bounceback.

Industries that suffer from Price Pressure Syndrome are those in which the value becomes negligible, and price is the only purchasing factor. Some examples are:

- Mattress Stores
- Basic Supermarkets
- Brick-and-Mortar Bookstores
- Furniture Stores

Additionally, telecommunication companies were stuck in this rut for some time. Using landlines, the only truly important feature was the ability to make a clear call. The advent and acceptance of cell phones allowed for a revolution in value: now, you must choose between phones, plans, and a variety of other factors.

How can you find out what factors are important to your clients? In the next chapter I'll talk about how to find out.

3

Ask Your Clientele

If you could ask your customers anything, what would you like to know? Are you concerned that your product's price point is too high? Do you want to know if your latest product offering or your company mission resonates with your customer? What value can you provide to your current and future clients that you do not even know about?

The good news is, you *can* ask them. Technology and social media have made it even easier to poll your audience. Listen to who is driving your business. By asking questions of the people with whom you make transactions, you can start identifying trends and quickly learn much about your industry and your own company. How do you get your customers' advice on finding a sweet spot?

Survey Says
Send out a survey to your consumer base to get their feedback on your business. If you have customer e-mails, there are many easy and affordable online survey services that allow you to build your own questions. You can then drill down into the information you would like to learn more about.

If you are concerned that people will not take the time to fill out a survey, try offering an incentive. You could create a contest that requires your customer fill out the survey to enter. Or offer a give-away or discount off a future purchase as a reward for completing the survey.

Ask the Experts

Another way to learn about customer interests would be to hear their questions. Plan an Ask the Expert Day where current and future clients call or e-mail questions that you and your staff answer.

Pay attention to the types of questions your customers are asking. What is this telling you about how they use your products or services? Are there common factors that are coming up? Can some of their issues be easily resolved or will they require major overhauls? Are they misunderstanding an aspect of your product? Is your branding leading them to feel like they don't relate to this service?

Share Your Findings

How else can you use those questions and answers you collect? If you see common threads, chances are, many of your customers have similar concerns and needs. Use the information to develop material that you share with your customers. The information can become the basis for your blog, your electronic newsletter, your article series, your collection of short online videos, and your podcast or executive audio series.

Section II –
Focus on Four Crucial Areas

4

Think Profitability

To narrow down your sweet spot, you need to focus on four essential areas. The first is profitability. This may seem obvious, but sometimes business owners confuse sales with profits. You can sell millions of units, but if you are not making a healthy margin on it, you will not make any money.

Don't waste time and resources on products or services that are dragging down your company. To find the sweet spot, you may have to make some cuts. At the end of the day, eliminating the baggage of a company's offerings can be a daunting task.

Keep in mind Pareto's Principle, commonly known as the 80/20 Rule of Business: 80 percent of profit comes from 20 percent of product. Spend some time figuring out which of your offerings and clientele actually gives you the greatest profits. Build a niche within your niche: evolving to assist profitable clients can lead you to continuously dominate the field.

Focus Bullseye

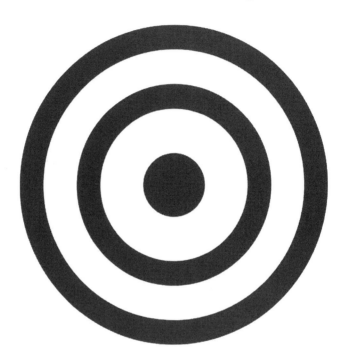

A company like Teledyne can serve as a warning for the 80/20 Rule. When founder and chairman Henry Singleton retired in 1989, Teledyne was operating in industries as unrelated as military weaponry and life insurance. They had not concentrated their efforts, and were stretched too thin.

Without Singleton to maintain the juggling act, Teledyne was subject to a series of takeovers, reorganizations, and acquisitions.

Only around 2011 had it regained the economic diversity and market interest it possessed over 20 years before. Although there are over 100 subsidies, the company website itself now promises to "serve niche market segments."

Sweet Spot Success: ServiceMaster

In 1929, ServiceMaster began as a moth proofing company in Chicago. Founder Marion E. Wade was a deeply religious man and this translated into an emphasis on honesty and customer service in his business.

This commitment to integrity and customer service continued as the business expanded. In the 1950s, the company began to offer carpet-cleaning services as one of the country's first franchise businesses. By the 1980s, they had expanded into a network of high quality home care services, including such high-profile brands as Terminix, TruGreen, American Home Shield, ServiceMaster Clean, Merry Maids, Furniture Medic, and AmeriSpec. They serve around 8 million customers every year across all their brands and have revenue of $10 billion.

With such a wide variety of offerings, it would be easy for ServiceMaster to suffer from a diluted brand. But regardless of the service being offered, there is a strong commitment to their key mission: "to simplify and improve the quality of our customers' lives." These services are the leaders in their categories, not because they are the cheapest, but because they are perceived as the best. Their customer's know the work will be done well and they will be treated fairly.

Rather than trying to compete with other services based on price and cutting their profit margins, ServiceMaster's focus on customer service allows them to remain profitable with a loyal customer base.

Sweet Spot Turned Sour: Failing to Find the Profit in Saturn

A perfect example of what can happen when you don't consider this aspect from the beginning is the sad story of Saturn. In 1991, General Motors created the brand as a response to the success of the low-priced and compact Japanese imports.

Saturn had all the makings of a great success story: it was an affordable, well-made, American car. While it was under the General Motors umbrella, it was leveraged as a separate entity with its own factories and dealerships to allow them to focus on the brand.

Saturn resonated with the customers who liked the simplicity of their method. When it launched, there was one model of car at a fixed price of less than $11,000. Buyers no longer had to haggle with dealers, never knowing if they had really gotten the best value. It was all there in black and white for them and they knew that they didn't need to shop around. What a revolutionary idea!

Their initial marketing strategy really focused on this revolution in car buying; their slogan was "A Different Kind of Car Company" and they emphasized that they were there for their customers. They had found their niche market – people who wanted a good deal but hated the hassle of negotiating. These customers valued simplicity and service and Saturn gave them just that.

Saturn also fostered a strong sense of customer loyalty through their maintenance plans. Their independent dealerships and factories allowed them to control all the aspects of the supply chain and customer service. Due to this, Saturn earned high rankings for customer satisfaction with repair services that placed them on par with luxury brands.

What went wrong? If they were hitting all those points, how did Saturn fail? GM did not adequately support the brand internally, which caused it to stagnate. What good is all that customer loyalty if you don't offer new models for them to buy? As a result, when other car companies were introducing larger models like SUVs and minivans, Saturn was losing ground. There was nothing new for the customer to "trade up" to and so they went elsewhere. Their sales peaked in 1994 and remained flat or down every year after that. GM reported at one point that they were losing $3000 on every model they sold.

Over the next 15 years, Saturn continued to flounder and attempted to reinvigorate its sales through new marketing. The efforts proved disappointing as the company jumped from one slogan to the next. They already had customer loyalty, so that wasn't the issue that needed fixing. They failed to seize upon how to translate their loyalty into profitability.

By 2009, as GM declared bankruptcy, it finally got rid of the Saturn brand along with its other unprofitable divisions, Pontiac and Oldsmobile. Despite its eventual failure, Saturn had elements of success that have been adopted by other companies. But remember that as you look for the sweet spot, you can't overlook the profitability factors. This needs to be a key element of your total package.

5

Leverage Your Value

The second critical area for finding the sweet spot is leveragability. Leverage in business is positional power. Like the mechanical advantage of a lever, business leverage is the ability to effectively improve and enhance your standing through the use of your current assets.

With leverage in mind, let us look at the offerings that your business has today, how much value is in them, and how much you can grow with your current offerings.

To do this, you need to answer the following two questions - and answer them honestly since you are the only one that knows.

1. What are you willing to give up?

2. What are you *not* willing to give up?

Again, the business owners I work with usually take out a calculator and start doing the math on percentages, revenue generated to date, or worse, they look at what they made last year.

If this is you, stop.

Instead, look at what future revenue you could drive with offering only what gives your clients the most value. Do you have a company value statement that describes your services and products?

My sweet spot advice: lose the rest so you can become the best at your core value offerings. Become the go-to company in your industry.

Less is more and it will always be that way.

The problem that is keeping you from the sweet spot and causing the value to be stuck inside your business is simply that you are probably not using all of these strategies enough to:

- Demonstrate your value (show, do not tell)
- Share value (no point keeping it hidden)
- Articulate value (articulation is key)
- Impress value (make it stick)

For most business owners, showcasing the value that they bring to their customers, clients, prospects, and internal and external stakeholders is just a dream. If you are like those entrepreneurs, the value in your company is never realized.

Why? Because it is not easy. The sweet spot solution lies deep in the company and you might never have done the work necessary to get it out in the open, where it can make you money.

So many dream. So few achieve.

Here is the secret I have learned after more than twenty-five years starting, building and selling businesses – my own and for my clients:

The Value in Your Business Is Not What You Think It Is

The underlying value of your products and services usually has more to do with the experience of buying and using them, rather than the product or service itself.

Let us examine an experience-driven company that many of us could not live with out.

This is the company that changed buying coffee from a commonplace task to an art form.

Obviously this is Starbucks, home of the $4 cup of coffee.

Starbucks has its own language that most of us now know and gladly use.

When Howard Schultz bought Starbucks, it was a small coffee company with one location in Seattle, Washington; he turned the idea of a coffee shop into an extraordinary coffee experience.

He set the stage for a new coffee shop atmosphere: where seating options include traditional tables and chairs and also comfortable living room chairs, where customers can settle in to relax over their drink.

Wi-Fi allows guests to bring computers and treat Starbucks as their temporary office where they can work or meet with colleagues and clients.

The Starbucks menu brought a new language where drinks are measured as tall, grande, and venti. Carefully selected music plays in the background.

Companies that enjoy outstanding success cater to a specific audience and create their own value proposition and their own language.

Are people willing to pay premium prices for the Starbucks experience? The answer is a resounding yes, and not only in the US but around the globe.

Starbucks coffee may or may not be subjectively good, but it is the Starbucks culture that truly makes it a valuable company.

In order to maximize your value, once you have established your experience asset, do not keep it a secret.

Make sure that:

- Customers and clients see it
- Banks see it
- Partners see it
- Suppliers see it
- Distributors, dealers, and resellers see it
- Franchisees see it

Sweet Spot Success: Marriott Brands

John Willard Marriott's first independent business venture was as a root beer vendor in Washington D.C. From this solitary shop, he expanded the line into a multi-state restaurant chain called Hot Shoppes.

The 1940s offered Marriott an opportunity to win contracts and make connections during the potent economic growth of the Second World War. While this aspect of his business was expanding, Marriott simultaneously began experimenting with motels and hotels in the Greater DC area.

The 1960s through the mid '80s were an era of innovation for the corporation. The blanket industry designation was "hospitality," but this entailed more than just hotels. They expanded into airline food and government cafeterias, international resorts and cruise ships.

Shortly before J.W. Marriott's death, the brand began to spread to accommodate specifically businessmen: the Courtyard designation was a quiet and professional hotel, for the traveling executive.

The success of the Courtyard logo led to a new corporate identity, "A Bed for Every Traveler." They opened a myriad of specific hotels, catered to different types of visitors. Included in this expansion were Fairfield Inns, TownePlace Suites, and a share of the luxurious Ritz-Carlton. Marriott continues to diversify and create a global product.

J.W. Marriott was a consummate opportunist. He created a culture of development while maintaining an overarching presence and warmth. His Hot Shoppes and its subsequent restaurant chain could surely have been enough to make Marriott a wealthy man; however, he saw markets where he could continue to succeed. It is said that Marriott tried to personally visit all of his enterprises to make sure they were up to his standards. In his book *The Spirit to Serve*, Marriott claimed that it was the *people*, not the *properties* that made his company thrive. If the employees did not believe in the product they were selling, then no customer ever could. Room redesigns, a mainstay of competitors, are less important for the company than proper and professional staffs or amenities.

This spirit has continued through the recession of the late 2000s. As of 2010, the Marriott group was the 3rd largest hotel chain in the world. They maintain an annual rate of growth of 4.7 percent, well above competitors in a difficult economy. Marriott has found its sweet spot in hospitality.

A final note about this corporation: as the 20th century came to a close, Marriott made a decision to move into a managerial role with its hotel chain. Each location is directly responsible to the central brand, rather than an independent franchise licensee. This is a company that takes its name and image very seriously. The Marriott sweet spot is one that its officers seek to protect.

Sweet Spot Gone Sour: I Hear Sears Is Having a Sale

Another value magnifier is to identify vertical markets you can cash in on. It is very hard to be the go-to company across all industries and for all sectors.

Sears started as a mail order catalog in the late 1800s. The first Sears retail store opened in 1925, and from the 1920s to the 1950s Sears built an empire of urban department stores. Starting in the 1950s the company expanded the empire into suburban markets, then malls in 1960s and 1970s. By the 1980s Sears was the largest retailer in the United States.

Unfortunately Sears forgot its sweet sport and became a conglomerate. Sears had formed Allstate insurance back in the 1930s, but in the 1980s they added Dean Witter financial services, Coldwell Banker real estate, started Prodigy as a joint venture with IBM, and introduced the Discover credit cards.

By the 1990s Sears began to divest much of its non-retail operations that were hurting its bottom line. The last sale Sears made was itself. In

November of 2004 Kmart announced its plans to purchase Sears. As a part of the purchase, the Kmart Holdings Corporation would change its name to Sears Holdings Corporation. The new corporation announced that it would continue to operate stores under both the Sears and Kmart brands.

6

Monitor Customer Resonance

One of the key ingredients to your sweet spot is finding a product or service that resonates with your customers. If your customers don't understand the deeper purpose behind your company, it will be hard for them to be passionate about what you are offering. How you communicate about your company makes a huge difference in connecting with your customer base.

Let's return to Steve Jobs and Apple for a moment. Apple's mission statement is succinct, broad, and reflects the company's products and goals.

Here it is in full:

Apple designs Macs, the best personal computers in the world, along with OS X, iLife, iWork and professional software. Apple leads the digital music revolution with its iPods and iTunes online store. Apple has reinvented the mobile phone with its revolutionary iPhone and App Store, and is defining the future of mobile media and computing devices with iPad.

Examine the powerful language that Apple, as a company, has chosen: words like "best," "leads," "reinvented," and "defining." This is an organization that can quickly describe what makes it a value, and what is the moneymaking sweet spot in which it operates.

Do not make prospective customers think. Just make sure they *get* it.

People Don't Buy What You Do; People Buy Why You Do It

About three and a half years ago I made a discovery. And this discovery profoundly changed my view on how I thought the world worked, and it even profoundly changed the way in which I operate in it. As it turns out, there's a pattern. As it turns out, all the great and inspiring leaders and organizations in the world – whether it's Apple or Martin Luther King or the Wright brothers – they all think, act, and communicate the exact same way. And it's the complete opposite to everyone else. All I did was codify it, and it's probably the world's simplest idea. I call it the golden circle.

Why? How? What? This little idea explains why some organizations and some leaders are able to inspire where others aren't. Let me define the terms really quickly. Every single person, every single organization on the planet knows what they do, 100 percent. Some know how they do it, whether you call it your differentiated value proposition or your proprietary process or your unique selling proposition (USP). But very, very few people or organizations know why they do what they do. And by "why"

I don't mean "to make a profit." That's a result. It's always a result. By "why," I mean: What's your purpose? What's your cause? What's your belief? Why does your organization exist? Why do you get out of bed in the morning? And why should anyone care? Well, as a result, the way we think, the way we act, the way we communicate is from the outside in. It's obvious. We go from the clearest thing to the fuzziest thing. But the inspired leaders and the inspired organizations – regardless of their size, regardless of their industry – all think, act, and communicate from the inside out.

Let me give you an example. I use Apple because they're easy to understand and everybody gets it. If Apple were like everyone else, a marketing message from them might sound like this: "We make great computers. They're beautifully designed, simple to use, and user friendly. Want to buy one?" "Meh." And that's how most of us communicate. That's how most marketing is done, that's how most sales is done, and that's how most of us communicate interpersonally. We say what we do, we say how we're different or how we're better, and we expect some sort of a behavior, a purchase, a vote, something like that. Here's our new law firm: We have the best lawyers with the biggest clients, we always perform for our clients who do business with us. Here's our new car: It gets great gas mileage, it has leather seats, buy our car. But it's uninspiring.

Here's how Apple actually communicates. "Everything we do, we believe in challenging the status quo. We believe in thinking differently. The way we challenge the status quo is

> by making our products beautifully designed, simple to use, and user friendly. We just happen to make great computers. Want to buy one?" Totally different right? You're ready to buy a computer from me. All I did was reverse the order of the information. What it proves to us is that people don't buy what you do; people buy why you do it.
>
> *- Simon Sinek, "How Great Leaders Inspire Action," TEDxPuget Sound*

Imagine you are alone in an elevator with a generous billionaire: over the course of the 30 seconds you have, how would you pitch your business? How can you take your hard work and turn it into a series of key phrases and ideas?

Think what can you do to go *deep* instead of broad with your value.

Once you have made that decision, to find the sweet spot, you must work on being able to do the following:

1. Spell out your value proposition in one sentence or less.

2. Deliver a specific type of value to a specific set of customers and prospects.

3. Articulate the message completely free of jargon.

What does this add up to? It means, as we say in Philly, use plain friggin' English. Just make it clear, powerful, and obvious.

Sweet Spot Success: American Express

Did you know that American Express has been around since the mid-19th century? To deliver its rich corporate history in entirety is better served for a full book. Instead, this case study will hit the critical junctures of the company's foundation.

American Express began in 1850 as a business completely separate from our contemporary understanding of its services. With the great westward expansion of the United States, American Express served as a private "express" service for moving money and valuables across the country. As the transportation infrastructure of the country grew, the demand for American Express stagecoaches started to wane. Railroads, larger (and safer) ships, and eventually motorized vehicles would supplant the horse-drawn business model of the company.

In 1890, CEO J.C. Fargo found that despite his pristine letters of credit, he could not get cash in many places in Europe. Within one year, American Express had taken Fargo's problem and turned it into a very profitable solution. They created and established the American Express Travelers Cheque, a monetary substitute guaranteed by the company itself. The concept worked: in 1891 (the first year), $9,120 of travelers cheques were sold. By 1913, the annual sales were approximately $32 million.

With nationwide fuel shortages during World War One, the United States government officially ended the "express" component of American Express. All domestic shipping was consolidated to one federal company, effectively forcing American Express out of its founding business. Fortunately, the company was rapidly becoming a world leader in the financial market.

The 1950s brought the advent of the other product typically associated with American Express: their line of charge cards. The company operated on an exclusive level, charging higher fees to both merchants and users. This concept has carried to the present day: the merchant rate for AmEx cards is almost one percent higher than their average competitors, and the intrigue of the Centurion Card's elite status has the wealthiest in the world carrying their cards.

Through the years, American Express has served as a reliable and prime choice in its industry. Their guaranteed service has always placed the company in a select class; the higher rates concur with higher anticipated benefits and amenities. The executives during the formative years were all deeply knowledgeable about the industry: the aforementioned J.C. Fargo, his brother William, and founding officer Henry Wells were also associated with the creation of the Wells Fargo brand.

Price, as this example shows, is just a single part of a company's value. American Express costs more and charges a fee to join, yet is still an industry leader. Finding the sweet spot sometimes takes a combination of a strong team and an understanding that, on occasion, serving less yields more.

Sweet Spot Gone Sour: Where Have You Gone, Wendy?

"When Dave Thomas opened our first Wendy's restaurant in 1969, he opened the door to a new gold standard in quality food," says the Wendy's official Website. The company states that his words "We don't cut corners on quality," affected everything from their hamburgers to their customer service. When other restaurants were using frozen beef and mass-producing food, Thomas developed an innovative method to prepare fresh, made-to-order hamburgers, allowing them to quickly serve high quality and variety to millions of customers daily. He coined the phrase, "Quality is our recipe."

In the case of Wendy's, the value was melted away by a loss of focus. Instead of remaining in its niche, the company tried to directly take on its competitors: McDonalds and Burger King. The consumer began to view Wendy's as a typical fast food joint. As a result, the quality of the product deteriorated, sales declined, and the value slipped away.

In 2012, Wendy's new CEO called the dour results of the past few years "self-inflicted wounds" and vowed to do better, laying out plans for reclaiming market share from higher-end burger competitors like Five Guys and Smashburger and fast-casual competitors like Panera and Chipotle.

The CEO said that the company's problems were its own fault. Though Wendy's had carved out a niche in the restaurant business as fast food for grown-ups, it had lost its way in recent years.

Remember that your customer's care about the purpose behind your products and they have to identify with it to truly hit that sweet spot.

7

The Riches Are In The Niches

A lot of companies manufacture high-tech glass, digital displays, and various screen technologies. Corning, however, has patented Gorilla Glass® and cornered the mobile phone market.

Corning has been in the glass business for over 100 years. For most of their other products, there are countless competitors; for Gorilla Glass, they dominate the field.

How does Gorilla Glass apply to your situation?

The final area to focus on is the marketability of your product or service. You need to carve out the right niche for your company and find a way to reach those targeted consumers.

I am sure to some of you, the idea of limiting the amount of people you are offering your product to does not sound like a recipe for success. But being able to focus in on the customers who will most benefit from your particular product or service will allow you to get more out of a smaller segment.

In an earlier section, I discussed that you may need to let some aspects of your business go. This will help you find the value in your company without the distractions of too many offerings taking away from the sweet spot.

Be a Category Killer
A Category Killer is a term for a company that has such a distinct competitive advantage, they essentially eliminate all the other market entities. Think of eBay, Toys R Us, Best Buy. They have little-to-no real competition.

How does a new contender take on established big shots? *By becoming a category killer.* Category killers try to elicit a certain response from clients and consumers. To do so, they build an experience from the ground up.

Is there an opportunity for you to become a category killer? Here are a few examples.

Sephora - Self Service With A Side of Luxury
LVMH, the parent company of Louis Vuitton luggage, is also responsible for the reigning royalty of cosmetics: Sephora. The company saw a fragmented market for its competitors and therefore an opportunity. As a luxury brand, they understood the importance of making customers feel special. When they purchased a popular French cosmetics company in the 1990s, they built upon the self-service model while increasing the

customer service element and expanding into new markets. By emphasizing personalized service, frequent samples, and high-quality giveaways, Sephora unified and won. They are the strongest competitor in the beauty industry and have strong brand recognition and loyalty from their customers.

Go Daddy – Outrageous Advertising and Excellent Customer Service

You may be most familiar with Go Daddy from their risque Super Bowl ads, but did you know they are a category killer? When Bob Parsons founded the company in 1999, no one expected anyone to be able to topple the domain registration giant Network Solutions. Yet through aggressive marketing campaigns and a comittment to low prices and great service, they are now the number one domain name registrar in the world.

According to their Website, Go Daddy currently registers, renews, or transfers a domain name more than every second of every day, has more than 9.5 million customers worldwide, manages more than 49 million domain names and employs more than 3,300 people. Go Daddy is also the largest Web hosting provider in the world with more than 5 million active hosting accounts.

In the next section, we'll talk more about how Parsons transformed his company into a category killer with just the right sweet spot.

Becoming a category killer is a sweet victory. Maintaining focus on the brand promise is what prevents the business from turning sour.

Sweet Spot Success: Federal Express

In 1965, Yale University undergraduate Frederick W. Smith wrote a term paper about the passenger route systems used by most airfreight shippers, which he viewed as economically inadequate. Smith wrote of the need for shippers to have a system designed specifically for airfreight that could accommodate time-sensitive shipments such as medicines, computer parts and electronics.

(Contrary to popular lore, he did not receive a C on the term paper. Smith once said he usually got C grades in college and thus the legend began.)

In August of 1971, following a stint in the Marine Corps, Smith bought controlling interest in Arkansas Aviation Sales, located in Little Rock, Arkansas. While operating his new firm, Smith identified the tremendous difficulty in getting packages and other airfreight delivered within one to two days. This dilemma motivated him to do the necessary research for resolving the inefficient distribution system. Thus, the idea for Federal

Express was born: a company that revolutionized global business practices and now defines speed and reliability.

According to the official company Website, Federal Express was so-named due to the patriotic meaning associated with the word "Federal," which suggested an interest in nationwide economic activity. At that time, Smith hoped to obtain a contract with the Federal Reserve Bank and, although the proposal was denied, he believed the name was a particularly good one for attracting public attention and maintaining name recognition.

The company incorporated in 1971 and officially began operations in 1973, with the launch of 14 small aircraft from Memphis International Airport. On that night, Federal Express delivered 186 packages to 25 U.S. cities from Rochester, NY, to Miami, FL.

Company headquarters were moved to Memphis, TN, a city selected for its geographical center to the original target market cities for small packages and its favorable flying weather.

The company also played a part in lobbying the government for the commercial use of cargo aircrafts, which would eventually make up the majority of the Federal Express fleet.

These business decisions were an essential part of Smith's plan. He named the company *Federal* Express with the implication of nation-wide expansion. Perhaps most important, the focus moved away from exclusively small documents and parcels: with its own cargo planes, Federal Express could ship any package across the country.

The early 1980s saw a slew of competitors making their way into the express parcel delivery niche. Federal Express responded by expanding its fleet and foraying into international delivery. From 1984 to 1995, the company began to acquire other networks and airlines to compete in Europe, Japan, and mainland Asia. This coincided with the rebranding of Federal Express to the current name of FedEx, as the company was no longer restricted to domestic deliveries.

How does FedEx maintain value for investors and customers?

Years before founding his business, Smith knew where to bring the value. He had identified a problem and built up the know-how and capital to solve it.

FedEx was an early adopter of new technology; they incorporated a computer model to increase efficiency, getting in on the ground-floor of spreadsheet calculations. By the time his niche market began to seem crowded with competition, Smith had already developed a scalable strategy to open up his company. While the first ten years featured no major mergers, the second decade of

FedEx focused on exclusive contracts, such as an acquisition that secured them as the sole United States package delivery system in China. The company also established a series of different delivery options to compete with the express services of the United States Postal Service; by 2001, the USPS had contracted FedEx to make all of their document deliveries for them.

The company's original slogan, "When it Absolutely, Positively has to be there overnight," fit the niche service that they offered. Since then, FedEx has expanded their value proposition to cover a full line of delivery services: Priority, Two-Day, and Standard.

The most recent phrasing of the slogan reflects the variety of products FedEx now presents: "The World On Time." The business has marketed itself to clients and stakeholders based on the knowledge and expansion of its own value.

The FedEx Corporation had a bottom line of $1.2 billion in 2011. This company has found its market and thrived, becoming a true captain of industry.

Sweet Spot Success: Toyota's Pursuit of Perfection with the Lexus

What do we know about Toyota? They produce dependable, mid-range cars with good gas mileage.

According to *The New York Times*, in 2008, Toyota had achieved its long-held goal of becoming the number one car maker in the world, passing General Motors, which had been the leader since 1931.

But in the late 1980s, Toyota executives had a different target in mind: the luxury market. Toyota created the Lexus brand to take on the deluxe imports like Mercedes and BMW. While the Japanese brand had made serious inroads into the American market, it was not viewed as high-end. To achieve this, they hoisted their sweet spot to this newer, more luxurious (and expensive) brand. The Lexus brand's first ad campaign ran under the following slogan: "The Relentless Pursuit of Perfection." This is a wonderfully evocative way for the Toyota/Lexus executives to say, "Watch out, we have a new goal!"

Toyota designed the modern dealership experience for its Lexus brand. Like a restaurant franchise, there was uniform, no-haggle pricing. Instead of fighting for commission, the sales people were on the floor trying to *educate* the consumer. These were luxury salesmen, not the tired stereotype of a car salesman.

The opposite situation happened to the car manufacturer Oldsmobile. When they attempted to enter the high-end market, their product failed.

The expensive Oldsmobile Aurora was placed right alongside less exclusive models. *Consumers could not tell the luxury from the generic.* It just did not feel like a special product.

Section III –
The Transformative Tool Chest

8

Tools to Cash In On Your Sweet Spot

The keys to transformative leadership are growth and change. As the leader, you will be shaping your business to bring out the best in what is there while making it into something new and better. In the same sense that you would never start to remodel a house without the right tools for the job, you must be equipped with a transformative tool chest to remodel your business.

As I have discussed before, it is crucial for an entrepreneur to move beyond just a great idea. You must have the leadership to guide your company to the next level and guide your employees to perform at their peak levels. But first, you must do a bit of self-reflection. The first set of tools are designed to help you understand yourself and your company better, so that you can lead the company effectively.

Tool 1: Finding Your Best Hats
As an idea person, it would be a wonderful luxury to be able to focus on your area of expertise and have everything else fall into place for your

company. But as entrepreneurs know all too well, they are responsible for many aspects of their business. I call these aspects the 12 hats of the entrepreneur.

1. **Administrative** – All the mundane tasks needed to keep your business running, such as maintaining proper insurances and licenses, or filing tax returns.

2. **Finance** – Everything money-related, such as collecting monies and accounts payables.

3. **Sales** – Everything related to sales and sales management.

4. **Marketing** – Everything to do with marketing of the business, such as advertising, events, and trade shows.

5. **Operations** – Everything to do with daily operations and services.

6. **Delivery** – All aspects of delivery of your product or service.

7. **Human Resources** – Employee related issues, including hiring and firing.

8. **Strategy** – Long-term planning for the direction of the business.

9. **Tactical Strategy** – Short-term planning for the business.

10. Vision – The big picture of what the business does.

11. Mission – What does the company stand for?

12. Execution – The ability to start and complete projects for the business.

Most likely, you have a part in each of these categories, whether you like it or not. But now is the time to think through your contributions to each of these areas. Which ones are you effective at? Which ones give you the most satisfaction? Which aspects would you really like to have off your plate?

Now, choose your top three hats. These will be the functions that you will focus on. You will likely find that more will be accomplished if you aren't constantly switching hats and attempting to be involved in every area. How can you do this though? What about the rest of the hats? You must maximize and empower your other employees to be covering these aspects of the business. We will address this more in the coming chapters.

Tool 2: What Is Your Corporate Culture?

In the same way that you must communicate to your customers the driving force behind your company in a way that resonates, you must also get that passion across to your employees. I will discuss more about engaging your staff in the next chapter, but this tool should be one you focus on as soon as possible.

Strong corporate cultures are shown to be more profitable than their competitors. In his book, *The Culture Cycle*, Harvard Business School Professor Emeritus James L. Heskett quantifies the impact of culture on performance; according to his research, 20-30 percent of the difference in performance between competitors can be attributed to a company with an effective culture versus one that is "culturally unremarkable."

"We know, for example, that engaged managers and employees are much more likely to remain in an organization, leading directly to fewer hires from outside the organization," Heskett writes in the book. "This, in turn, results in lower wage costs for talent; lower recruiting, hiring, and training costs; and higher productivity (fewer lost sales and higher sales per employee). Higher employee continuity leads to better customer relationships that contribute to greater customer loyalty, lower marketing costs, and enhanced sales."

I can't tell you what your corporate culture ought to be. Just like the secret sauce that makes your product or service great, each culture is different. But, it is important that you identify and reinforce what your culture is (or what you want it to be).

In a post on the *Harvard Business Review Blog*, James Coleman identifies these six common components of great corporate cultures. Think about how these relate to your own culture.

1. Vision – This is your vision or mission statement. Use this as your starting point – this is the purpose behind your organization.

2. Values – The core values of your organization will guide the outlook of your employees as they work to achieve the vision.

3. Practices – The vision and values don't matter much if they are not put into practice. If you say one thing and do another, your culture will suffer.

4. People – The people in your organization have to share the values of the company or the culture will never be more than words.

5. Narrative – What is your unique story and how did it shape your organization?

6. Place – Don't take for granted the seemingly superficial aspects of your workplace – the aesthetics and feeling of the environment you work in have a major effect on culture.

A good example of a company with an extremely strong corporate culture is Disney. They reinforce their values consistently across every member of the company. So whether you are selling or are an executive in the corporate office, you feel part of the same group. It is part of their management strategy at every level and every stage of recruitment and development.

The Disney Career's Website describes their culture this way:

Each of our companies has a unique ability to harness the imagination in a way that inspires others, improves lives across the world and brings hope, laughter and smiles to those who need it most. Together as one team, we embrace the values that make The Walt Disney Company an extraordinary place to work:

Innovation
We are committed to a tradition of innovation and technology.

Quality
We strive to set a high standard of excellence.

We maintain high-quality standards across all product categories.

Community

We create positive and inclusive ideas about families.

We provide entertainment experiences for all generations to share.

Storytelling

Timeless and engaging stories delight and inspire.

Optimism

At The Walt Disney Company, entertainment is about hope, aspiration and positive outcomes.

Decency

We honor and respect the trust people place in us.

Our fun is about laughing at our experiences and ourselves.

These values live in everything we do. They create a unified mission that all our people believe in and work toward.

Disney is so skilled at creating a corporate culture that translates into profits and extreme brand loyalty that they started a business training course called the Disney Institute (see box at the end of the next chapter).

Another excellent example is the Ritz-Carlton hotel brand. They call their corporate philosophy the Gold Standards and they strive to make sure every employee embodies it and passes that experience along to the customers.

Here are the elements of the Gold Standards (from their Website). Notice that it is a two-way street – they expect high standards from their employees, but they also make a promise to them to value them and help them grow within the company.

The Credo
The Ritz-Carlton Hotel is a place where the genuine care and comfort of our guests is our highest mission.

We pledge to provide the finest personal service and facilities for our guests who will always enjoy a warm, relaxed, yet refined ambience.

The Ritz-Carlton experience enlivens the senses, instills well-being, and fulfills even the unexpressed wishes and needs of our guests.

Motto
At The Ritz-Carlton Hotel Company, L.L.C., "We are Ladies and Gentlemen serving Ladies and Gentlemen." This motto

exemplifies the anticipatory service provided by all staff members.

Three Steps Of Service

A warm and sincere greeting. Use the guest's name.

Anticipation and fulfillment of each guest's needs.

Fond farewell. Give a warm good-bye and use the guest's name.

Service Values: I Am Proud To Be Ritz-Carlton

I build strong relationships and create Ritz-Carlton guests for life.

I am always responsive to the expressed and unexpressed wishes and needs of our guests.

I am empowered to create unique, memorable and personal experiences for our guests.

I understand my role in achieving the Key Success Factors, embracing Community Footprints and creating The Ritz-Carlton Mystique.

I continuously seek opportunities to innovate and improve The Ritz-Carlton experience.

I own and immediately resolve guest problems.

I create a work environment of teamwork and lateral service so that the needs of our guests and each other are met.

I have the opportunity to continuously learn and grow.

I am involved in the planning of the work that affects me.

I am proud of my professional appearance, language and behavior.

I protect the privacy and security of our guests, my fellow employees and the company's confidential information and assets.

I am responsible for uncompromising levels of cleanliness and creating a safe and accident-free environment.

The Employee Promise

At The Ritz-Carlton, our Ladies and Gentlemen are the most important resource in our service commitment to our guests.

By applying the principles of trust, honesty, respect, integrity and commitment, we nurture and maximize talent to the benefit of each individual and the company.

The Ritz-Carlton fosters a work environment where diversity is valued, quality of life is enhanced, individual aspirations are fulfilled, and The Ritz-Carlton Mystique is strengthened.

Take a moment to codify your corporate culture and use the six areas described above as a guideline. Note if there are areas that are not currently strongly articulated that need to be reinforced with your staff. You may want to take the time to refine this to simple statements like the examples above. This will help guide team members now and will be a helpful recruitment tool later.

Tool 3: Test and Test Again

Sometimes it may seem that as you refine your product or service to find the Sweet Spot that you must get everything perfect before releasing it. But this is a miscalculated strategy. As the saying goes, "Perfect is the enemy of good."

If you wait until everything is just right, you may miss your window of opportunity. Furthermore, you may be failing to foresee problems that will arise in the testing phase that can be avoided later. This will also allow you to understand the marketability of your product. Have you found the right market? If not, you can adjust while still developing and not wasting time.

This can be a major problem with emerging technologies. If you have a jump on a technology, you must push your company to truly own the market. As you will see from the following story of RCA and LCD screens, sometimes failure to evolve and change will lead to losing the race to market. This story is an example of the type of attitude that is totally unacceptable in a transformative leader. The top people at RCA could not see the potential in front of them and let this revolutionary technology slip away. RCA was a company that had been on the forefront of radio and television technologies, but they got comfortable and failed to innovate.

Sweet Spot Gone Sour – Lessons to be Learned from RCA and LCD

Liquid Crystal Display (LCD) technology was discovered in the 1960s at the RCA Laboratories. Despite having the jump on the technology, RCA did not devote the resources to it that would have been necessary to take it to the next level. Instead, the true product developments were made by Japanese and European companies and would take another 25 years to get to market. The following is excerpted from Hirohisa Kawamoto, "The History of Liquid-Crystal Displays," PROCEEDINGS OF THE IEEE, VOL. 90, NO. 4, APRIL 2002

The device was drawing a very small electric current, less than a microwatt of power per square centimeter and they were switching color with voltages substantially smaller than those of CRTs–less than 10 V for liquid-crystal dye mixture versus more than 1000 V for CRTs. This was in the fall of 1964. [The inventor, George] Heilmeier thought a wall-sized flat-panel color TV was just around the corner. As we will see, that realization took another quarter century.

When Heilmeier demonstrated this effect within the laboratories, the people there became excited. Vladimir Zworkin, known to many in the field as the father of television, heard about the experiment and summoned Heilmeier to his office to find out why people in the laboratories were so excited. Heilmeier explained how he had "stumbled" onto the guest-host color switching effect. He never forgot Zworkin's reflective reply: "Stumbled perhaps, but to stumble, one must be moving."

Alphanumeric displays, windows with electronically controlled transparency, static pictorial displays, an all electronic clock with a liquid-crystal readout, and liquid-crystal cockpit displays were fabricated. These crude prototypes excited everyone at RCA.

On May 28, 1968, RCA held a press conference at its headquarters at Rockefeller Plaza, New York. They proudly announced the discovery of a totally new type of electronic display. The display was dramatically different from traditional CRTs. It was lightweight, consumed little electrical power, and was very thin. The press conference drew the attention of scientific and industrial communities all over the world. This announcement initiated the development of digital watches in the U.S.,

Japan, and Germany and the work on pocket calculators in Japan. At the same time, it led to further scientific work in Germany, Switzerland, and the U.K.–particularly for the synthesis of new liquid-crystal materials suitable for use in display applications.

Naturally, Heilmeier wanted to see his invention evolve into RCA products. He went to company headquarters and convinced RCA to go into the business of LCDs. The task was given to the Solid-State Division in Sommerville, NJ, which was responsible for the design and production of semiconductor devices. However, Heilmeier quickly received negative responses from the naysayers. Liquid crystals were not "silicon." They were "dirty" by semiconductor standards. They were liquids. They were too easily duplicated. They were said to be too difficult to make. These were some of the many reasons the product division gave for its failure to commercialize LCDs.

At the time, RCA owned a substantial amount of business in CRTs [Cathode Ray Tubes, used in traditional televisions]. Top management eventually rejected the idea of LCDs because they represented a threat to their existing CRT business.

According to Heilmeier: "The people who were asked to commercialize (the technology) saw it as a distraction to their main electronic focus." In 1970, he gave up, accepting an appointment as a White House Fellow working in the Department of Defense as a Special Assistant to the Secretary of Defense.

Heilmeier's dream of a wall-hanging television in 1964 finally became a reality after a quarter of a century. In The Wall Street Journal, Heilmeier remarked: "I think you need to give the credit to the people who persevered and worked on LCDs for 25 years. I don't spend too much time wringing my hands about it, but I have a lot of satisfaction knowing we had the same vision in the 1960s."

9

Tools to Guide the Team

Now that you've narrowed down what product or service will be your company's Sweet Spot, it is likely you will need to make changes to align the team with the new focus. As a Transformative Leader, it is your role to be the agent of change in your organization. Most likely you are a small business owner and may not have the resources to start fresh and hire new top-level talent.

In order to get the most out of your company, you will need to take an active part in guiding, training, and managing your team. If you have assembled your toolbox, you will have all the resources you need to help the transformation run smoothly.

Tool 4: Evaluate Your Team

As you begin to shape the future of your company, you need to take the time to evaluate your overall goals and the current team members. Are all your employees in the right position? Are they being used effectively? Is there potential for changes that would benefit the team?

First, think about your overall vision for the future of the company and how you plan to transform it as you get to your Sweet Spot goals. For each of the transformative goals, list the tasks that will be required to achieve those goals. What skills are required for each of the tasks you listed? Be as specific as you can be with this list. Be sure to think back to your list of 12 hats – make sure the 9 remaining hats are being adequately covered on the list.

Now take a look at each of your employees. For each person, list their strongest skills in the workplace and whatever specialized training they might have.

You now have two lists that you can match against one another. This list may help you realize that certain members of your team are not being effectively used. Perhaps they are wasting time with tasks that are below their skill level and could be put to better use with a different focus. Or you could have a team member struggling with a task that could be more effectively handled by someone else.

In a perfect world you'd have a perfect fit, but that isn't likely to be the case. Instead, I bet that you have a number of overlaps and a number of gaps. Overlaps are a good problem to have – you can decide whether it is best to assign tasks to the most specialized person for the job or have them covered by the lowest level employee capable of handling them. Depending on the importance of the task, you can decide whether the quality of the work or the efficiency and cost is the primary criteria.

Gaps are a more complicated issue to solve. As you look through the list of employee skills, there may be some that could fill these gaps if they were adequately trained for the new task. If that is a possibility, this may be a quicker and more efficient way to fill this gap than looking outside your organization. In the next chapter, I will discuss how to recruit employees if you find you need to build up your team.

Tool 5: Clearly Communicate Changes

The next steps you take will determine your success in acting as a transformative leader. People are often resistant to change and may not react well to their jobs being shuffled around. It is crucial that these changes be communicated extremely clearly. You must take the lead in managing these changes and ensuring that everyone understands the reasons behind them and their place in the overall team.

With the entire staff, discuss the changes you hope to enact as part of your new initiatives to grow the company and reach the Sweet Spot that will help you all succeed. Then discuss the role changes with individual employees. For each person, their new role should be defined in writing. The new job description should include their specific tasks and responsibilities, who they report to, and anyone they oversee. It should all be articulated as clearly as possible so there is no confusion.

If you properly convey the benefit to the overall team and tie this into the corporate culture as a whole, your team will be motivated to work hard for the organization.

Tool 6: Empower Your Team

Now that you have aligned employees into the best positions for the overall organization, you must empower them to work effectively on its behalf. If you give employees the tools and authority to make decisions, then they will feel a responsibility to the organization and a desire to help it succeed.

Are there any obstacles that are keeping people from taking pride in their work or initiative in the workplace? What types of incentives could you provide to get your employees to be more in line with the corporate culture you are trying to reinforce?

On a related note, you must provide opportunities for your employees to grow and evolve with the company. Do employees feel that they can advance in the organization? If you are not making it clear that members of your team will be able to move up in their careers, they may look elsewhere.

Again, Disney is a great example of this type of motivation. The Disney Institute describes it this way: "Gratitude improves attitude. That's one reason why Disney leaders convey sincere appreciation, empathy and support to every Cast Member. They recognize accomplishments, involve Cast in developing customer service strategies, and give them the opportunity to make the best use of their talents and skills. It's a mutually beneficial practice—leaders create a better working relationship, employees understand their value to the company and, ultimately, our Guests receive the benefits of quality service."

It is possible though, that someone on your team is not performing well. Perhaps they are not understanding the changes or they are not working well within the team. In any case, as the leader you must take an active role in dealing with these issues. Allowing this type of issue to continue sets a bad example for other employees and may even get in the way of their work.

Speak with the employee about the problem and again be very clear in your communication. Try to listen and understand what they feel is going wrong, but then give direction on how to correct their problem going forward. You should be fair, but if you have to address the same issue repeatedly, you may need to remove the person from the team.

Disney's Approach to Leadership Excellence

Creating a significant change in an organization begins with a clear vision of the future, rooted in core values and communicated with passion. Drawing on decades of storytelling heritage, a Disney leader shares the vision in a way that makes an emotional connection and motivates action.

Disney has a foundation created by a strong heritage, established traditions, quality standards, and shared values. At each and every Disney Destination around the world, these are the assets that create our road map–the corporate culture that defines our people management processes and the philosophy that leads to every business decision. Upon this foundation we have built unique traits and behaviors, and introduced language, symbols, processes, and styles that distinguish us in the marketplace. By protecting and nurturing these differences, we remain committed, focused, and ready to achieve new business goals.

Disney leaders recognize that the values and behaviors they demonstrate day-to-day will be remembered longer than their accomplishments. With the ability to influence those around them, leaders need to live the values of the organization on a daily basis. Not only does this reveal what they personally value, it provides insight into their character and ensures that their leadership will have a long-lasting, positive impact.

–Disney Institute Courses

Southwest Airlines is a company known for treating their employees well and empowering them to be able to do what is best for the company and the customers. In the lobby of their Dallas headquarters, there is a huge inscription on the wall that reads:

> *The People of Southwest Airlines are the creators of what we have become—and of what we will be. Our People transformed an idea into a legend. That legend will continue to grow only so long as it is nourished—by our People's indomitable Spirit, boundless energy, immense goodwill, and burning desire to excel. Our thanks—and our love—to the People of Southwest Airlines for creating a marvelous Family and a wondrous airline!*

Southwest Airlines – Leading with Love

We empower our People to use common sense and good judgment. Yes, we have written rules and procedures, and you can go look at them, but I say to our folks every day, "The rules are guidelines. I can't sit in Dallas, Texas, and write a rule for every single scenario you're going to run into. You're out there. You're dealing with the public. You can tell in any given situation when a rule should be bent or broken. You can tell because it's simply the right thing to do in the situation you are facing."

Our folks are marvelous about handling all kinds of situations with our Customers. For example, we have had Pilots pay for hotel rooms because our Customers were getting off at different cities than they intended for the night, and the Pilots could see that the people needed help. They don't call and ask, "Is it okay? Will I get reimbursed?" They do these things because that's the kind of People they are.

When our People realize they can be trusted and they're not going to get called on the carpet because they bend or break a rule while taking care of a Customer–that's when they want to do their best. Our People understand that as long as the Customer Service decisions they make are not illegal, unethical, or immoral, they are free to do the right thing while using their best judgment–even if that means bending or breaking a rule or a procedure in the process. Servant Leadership and empowering your People is not soft management; it is management that not only gets great results but generates great human satisfaction for both our Employees and our Customers.

– Colleen Barrett, President Emeritus of Southwest Airlines Co., excerpted from *Lead With LUV,* 2010

10

Tools to Build the Team

As you go through the exercises I talked about in the previous chapter, you may find that there are certain gaps that need to be filled that will require outside recruitment. Recruitment is often labor intensive, expensive, and slow. In the end, you may end up with someone that isn't as good as they seemed initially.

How can you avoid these pitfalls? There are tools to help you find the right fit for your organization and then incorporate them smoothly into your current team.

Tool 7: Prioritize the Search

If you have properly implemented the steps from the previous chapter, you will know that the right people in the right job is extremely beneficial to the individual and the team as a whole. It is also a major problem to have someone that does not fit with your corporate culture or the team. So it is worth taking the time to get it right.

Be sure you have allotted enough time so that you can find the best person for the position without feeling pressured to choose someone too quickly.

GoDaddy is a major employer and they have hired nearly 1500 people in the last few years. In an interview with *Inc. Magazine*, their chief human resources officer, Lane Jarvis, discussed her recruiting strategies. Her advice was to realize that every employee was an important hire and to try to forecast hiring needs early in order to get ahead of it and not rush.

"Your customers are your most vital resource and you work really hard to get them," she told *Inc.* "Remember that every employee is going to touch a customer in some way, so you are putting your customers at risk by hiring a bad candidate."

Tool 8: Craft the Job Description

If you are filling a newly discovered job gap in your company, you will likely have to start from scratch with the job description. But even if you are filling a prior position, resist the urge to re-use old materials for expediency. Really examine what types of tasks you will expect this new employee to be responsible for and what skills will be necessary to do that. Be honest about what is expected from the position – you want the person applying to be fully aware of the situation so neither of you is disappointed later.

The corporate culture statement you worked on in the last chapter will be helpful here as well. Be sure that the candidates understand the core values of your organization. This will help you find people who are not only capable of completing the tasks at hand, but will have the right attitude to help take your company to the next level. You want employees who are excited to be a part of your team because they believe in what you do and the why behind it. Without that, there will be little satisfaction on either side.

Hire People Who Believe What You Believe

If you don't know why you do what you do, and people respond to why you do what you do, then how will you ever get people to vote for you, or buy something from you, or, more importantly, be loyal and want to be a part of what it is that you do. Again, the goal is not just to sell to people who need what you have; the goal is to sell to people who believe what you believe. The goal is not just to hire people who need a job; it's to hire people who believe what you believe. I always say that, you know, if you hire people just because they can do a job, they'll work for your money, but if you hire people who believe what you believe, they'll work for you with blood and sweat and tears.

– Simon Sinek, "How Great Leaders Inspire Action," TEDxPuget Sound

---

Tool 9: Finding The Right People

Again, Disney is a master at this type of thing. They call their human resources "casting" and they are looking for what they call "Right-Fit Talent." The Disney Institute describes it this way: "What good is aptitude without the right attitude? At Disney, we cast for candidates not just to fill a position, but to fulfill high standards. When making decisions that ensure we're finding the right person for the right role in scores of divisions and hundreds of departments and teams, our employment operation, Disney Casting, must answer the needs of our Guests, our leaders, our Cast Members, and our management. Why? It's a further reflection of the philosophy that defines our organization's culture and strategy."

GoDaddy is another example of a company that knows how to hire to fit their culture and vision. They provide easy to use web products but what sets them apart is their commitment to excellent customer service; in fact half of the over 3,000 employees work in customer service. But this commitment extends into their corporate culture beyond people who work specifically in their support centers. Since many customer issues must be dealt with by the IT staff, they are trained to also make customer service a priority. The wider company culture is crucial at all levels and a poor hiring fit has the potential to damage their reputation.

Have Faith in Your People

It's very important that our employees understand the "why" of the work they do. When my team logs into a server they know that they are touching customers' websites, and that their actions (good or bad) directly impact those customers' livelihoods. So, they approach every task with the needs of those customers in mind. Helping your IT staff understand the scope and impact of what they do, as well as the value it brings to customers, helps build job satisfaction, because everyone wants to see that their job is important.

Giving my team the objective of providing world class hosting services, and then having faith that they will do the right thing, sounds obvious. But, I think a lot of IT leaders have a hard time with this. If I can't trust every single member of my team to do the right thing for our customers, for the right reasons, the problem doesn't rest with them, it rests with me as a leader. Sometimes you have to ask yourself hard questions and make hard decisions when you don't feel you can trust a member of your team. But, failing to do so hurts everyone in the long run. When you can place this kind of faith in your people, not only is life easier for you as a leader, but you'll find your team impresses you on a daily basis with their dedication and ingenuity.

Aside from the obvious fact that every business exists to provide value to its customers, giving an IT Operations team a customer service focus will ultimately help drive employee satisfaction as well. I know this from experience! My job as the head of Hosting Operations isn't to manage the operations team, it's to support them. Supporting the world's largest paid hosting provider is no small undertaking. But, our IT professionals are up to the challenge because they know how important their roles are to Go Daddy and to our customers!

– Cedar Coleman, "It's All About Customer Service," *Inside Go Daddy*

11

Keep Your Tools at the Ready

As a transformative leader, you must keep your business moving. You are not going to simply make one change and be set for life. This is a constant process that will require evaluation, adjustments, and continual innovation. Remember the tools I've discussed so far and keep using them to guide you through the journey.

The Disney Institute put it very succinctly: "Change doesn't happen overnight. On the way to the goal, it's easy for the group to get distracted and forget what they originally set out to do. Commitment is the bridge that connects the leader's vision with measureable impact on the organization. Committing to results involves a set of day-to-day strategies to focus attention and build momentum to real achievement."

Keeping the Sweet Spot Sweet – Evaluating the Business

Using a visual road map is a powerful way for you and your team to stay on track. I call this the 120-Day Snapshot. First, set several goals for the next

120 days. These can tie into your longer-term goals, but they are intended to be short-term things that can be accomplished in 4 months time. Now identify specific tasks and outcomes will allow you to reach those goals and decide how long each task should take.

Now draw this out as a map from task to task to reach the goal. There is no right way to visualize this; it can be as simple as arrows on a board with tasks under each arrow with an expected time line. You can customize it for each team member or make it a public company-wide snapshot. Either way, it should be clear and easy for people to read.

Every month, take a "snapshot" evaluation to establish the progress. Meet with the team and discuss which tasks have been accomplished, which things have taken longer than expected, and which things may not even need to be there at all. Be sure everyone on the team understands their roles and is working to make progress toward the goal.

An important thing to remember is that not all outcomes have to be home runs. In baseball, hitting singles consistently can be even more important than being able to hit a show-stopping home run now and then. Remind your team that sometimes singles are the way you get there – there is a "good enough" point that will get your task accomplished and move you towards your goal.

Reward Innovation

Innovation is a major component of being a trans-formative leader. Do not let yourself, or your company, get too comfortable. If you stop innovating, you will get left behind. You will lose your competitive edge and soon, your customers. Innovation is not just about the product itself – keep the customer experience in mind. Even if you are not coming out with revolutionary technologies, your business can be innovative. Use the following areas to guide your company.

Think about using technology to your advantage. There are many new "smart systems" to help you keep track of your business and customers in expanded ways. An excellent example is United Parcel Service (UPS), which created its own tracking codes to help sort packages for delivery, ensuring that the most efficient route is being used. And part of that efficiency is a simple, yet innovative idea: right-turn routes. The UPS trucks save time and gas by turning right about 90 percent of the time. Innovation does not have to be complicated to be great.

Customer Relationship Management (CRM) systems, usually a software or subscription service, can organize, automate, and synchronize sales, marketing, customer service, and technical support. These systems track data about your customers to help you improve your interactions with them and keep ahead of any issues they might be experiencing. Here are a couple of particularly helpful reports:

- DOA (Dead on Arrival) Report – a report on the products or services that get the most complaints or returns over errors. This will help you understand what isn't working and what is annoying your customers.

- Top Quality Problems Report – similarly, this report tells you which items have high service costs – there may be a service problem you do not know about that is costing you money.

- Most Profitable Service Offering – a report on the profitability of your offerings, which goes back to our discussion of the key elements in uncovering your Sweet Spot.

Use CRM to help identify areas of the customer experience where you could innovate. What can you do to exceed the expectations of your customers? Make sure they are being continually engaged by your company. Everyone loves upgrades – is there something you can provide that is an upgrade or add-on to something they have already purchased from you? Think outside the box on how to keep your customers happy and interacting with your company.

In the last two chapters, I talked about team development. Remember that innovation does not stop
with your products or services. It should include
your employees as well. You should do the exercise of evaluating your business needs against
your employee skills on a regular basis. If there is a
need for adjustments or specialized training, you
can be quick to make those changes.

Remember to reward every milestone for your
employees with lots of recognition. This does not
need to be financial in nature; many surveys of
employees have found that they actually get more
satisfaction out of a job where they feel appreci-
ated and valued, as opposed to just financially
compensated. As the company achieves goals, on
the snapshot evaluations or at other points of success, be sure to let those employees know that you
think they are doing a great job and appreciate
their contributions to the team. And if someone in
your company is responsible for innovative ideas,
be sure this is being recognized and rewarded so
as to encourage it in others as well.

Be sure you are going back to your tools each
time you need to hire a new employee. Take the
time to craft the job description and really look
for the right fit to your corporate culture. When
new hires start, do not just throw them into the
water. Establish training and mentoring that will
allow them to acclimate and really be integrated

into the company. And although it is unpleasant to do so, do not be afraid to fire someone that is not working out. Expecting someone to change and dragging out the inevitable will only lead to more problems for you.

Hire Slow, Fire Fast

If a person that you hire is not working out, don't hesitate to move on quickly. Especially if the employee is hurting productivity.

I know many businesses that took time to try and change someone. I haven't seen it be successful. People don't change. If someone is damaging the organization then they are hurting the environment that you are trying to build. That creates trust issues and you may lose good employees because of it. I look at it like a virus that can spread quickly and really hurt your bottom line.

That's why I follow the advice of hire slow and fire fast.

If you do fire someone make sure that you debrief your team and communicate the situation. Figure out what when wrong so that it won't happen again.

- Patrick Hull, Forbes.com

Cash In on Your Sweet Spot

When you are ready to sell your business – or get investors – you have to be able to present the current value *and* the future value of what you have built.

But rather than consider this "cash in" phase as the end, consider how you might utilize your investors' expertise – and money – to grow your business.

Think of it as a collaborative effort where these outside investors or new owners will do their very best to use *your* compass and map to navigate the business to where *they* want to go.

Although this may sound odd – or even disempowering – to you, the business owner, this is how value is "cashed in" and this is how it is supposed to work.

Here is an example. Groupon was offered $6 billion in a buyout offer from Google.

Why? Because they served a unique niche that was being underserved.

It was a scalable model that allowed Google to tie their brand into it and provide plentiful cross-marketing opportunities.

Bottom line: Google would have a higher value perception with Groupon than without them.

Google was being careful and highly selective with growing their value for their particular client base.

Groupon declined the investment and only time will tell if their value as a standalone company will go up or down. Experience would indicate that they may never get such a good deal to "cash in" again, but I would love to be wrong on this one.

Fact is, 90 percent of small and medium size businesses that are sold are asset sales – that means they are buying physical assets, not the brand or the customers or the value.

What a shame and what a lost opportunity to cash in big-time. The specialized product your company offers might not always work. Look to the future, and look to scale your ideas into the future!

Why does business failure happen so often? Because no value was created and thus none can be transferred. If you do not demonstrate and articulate value in a financial way, it will not magically show up when it is time to sell.

As an exercise to get you thinking in this new way, look outside of your own industry for examples and models of how to do this.

Are you in a service business? Look to product companies.

Are you in the product world? Look at web-based businesses.

Cross-pollinate ideas from banking, finance, technology, retail, consulting, engineering, travel, food, consumer goods, professional services, publishing, and other models that may be radically different from what you are comfortable and familiar with.

Run your business like the next guy and you will be stuck in the same loop as him.

Escape the "me too" trap: even the best must exit or retire when the time and circumstances are right.

When you first begin a business, you *are* the business. Remember to plan ahead for when you no longer need to, or perhaps no longer want to, be the head honcho.

Business owners who cash in big are the ones that throw off value independently of their personal time, attention, and presence.

"Cash in on the value" is really about three things:

1. **How do you get vendors and banks and stakeholders to give you more?** More cash, more marketing, more help, more partnership, and more resources

2. **How do you get your clients to give you more business?** Companies that fully cash in on their value are able to sell more, more often, and get customers to enthusiastically refer others.

3. **How do you create the life you always wanted?** If you are immersed 24/7 in your business, how do you structure that for your new lifestyle? Think about bringing in new management, delegating more, bringing in partners, hiring new staff; build the company around the value... *not* around you!

How Would You Answer?

As we've reached the end of the book, it will be helpful to review some of the major concepts and get started evaluating your company.

I now give you permission to write in this book. Use these pages to write down your answers and thoughts.

1. What is a sweet spot company that you admire?

_____

_____

_____

_____

_____

_____

2. How do they bring value to their clientele?

_____

_____

_____

_____

_____

3. In what "market" is my business? Against whom am I competing?

_____

_____

_____

_____

_____

4. What stage on the Simons Circle am I in right now?

_____

_____

_____

_____

_____

5. What is the greatest asset that I bring to my clients and customers?

_____

_____

_____

_____

6. What are some additional services or products that I know could help my clients that I am not offering today?

_____

_____

_____

_____

_____

7. Whom could I partner with or buy those services or products from that would complement what I do offer?

_____

_____

_____

_____

8. What is an experience-driven company that you like?

_____

_____

_____

_____

9. How could you improve the customer experience at your company?

_____

_____

_____

_____

These last five questions are not going to be answered in a few lines. My hope is that you use this book to get clarity about your business and its sweet spot. Take a moment to reflect on the following questions. Then take action.

1. How do you bring your secret sauce to your current business to tap fully into its value?

2. What is next and how do you leverage that same drive and energy into your next entrepreneurial venture?

3. What resources, tools, allies, and advocates do you need on your team to make this process as painless as possible?

4. Do you have a dream team already assembled that can help you think through some or all of these ideas?

5. When will you make the time to sit down and create a concrete game plan so when an opportunity arises to bring the value, you are not caught flat-footed?

The longer you are in business, the more important it is to hold true to your mission statement. *Big changes yield big results, and not always positive ones.* Some changes are inevitable; over the years, leadership (to a certain extent) will turn over. The focus needs to remain personal to you, the business owner. Profit margin is definitely an important facet of business, but it cannot overtake the founding ideals of the company.

References

Collins, James C. *Good to Great: Why Some Companies Make the Leap-and Others Don't*. New York, NY: HarperBusiness, 2001. Print.

"FedEx Annual Revenue Rises to $39.3 Billion." *Journal of Commerce*. Trade News. 05 Mar. 2012.

"History of FedEx Operating Companies." *About FedEx*. FedEx Express. Web. 05 Mar. 2012. <http://about.van.fedex.com/fedex-opco-history>.

Koch, Richard. *The 80/20 Principle: The Secret of Achieving More with Less*. New York: Currency, 1999. Print.

Mason, R. O., J. L. McKenney, W. Carlson, and D. Copeland. "Absolutely, Positively Operations Research: The Federal Express Story." *Interfaces* 27.2 (1997): 17-36. Print.

Rexrode, Christina. "Wendy's CEO: Our wounds were 'self-inflicted.'" Associated Press, 30 Jan. 2012

"Teledyne Founder Eases Up." *New York Times* 28 Apr. 1989, Business Day sec.

"Toyota Motor Corporation 2012 Earnings," *New York Times*, 5 Nov. 2012, Business Day section.

About the Author

Scott Simons is an accomplished entrepreneur, venture investor, company advisor, and speaker. Scott works closely with passionate entrepreneurs through his consulting company, the CEO Council and the Institute For Entrepreneurship, which he founded to bring business owners together to learn new ideas and share their experiences, growing larger enterprises.

Scott founded his first company, Simons Optical, at the age of 21. He went on to build several multi-million dollar enterprises. During the time he built his companies, he worked closely with private investment bankers and served as the Chair of the Council of Growing Companies, Pennjerdel Chapter, where he learned the inner workings of corporate America through exposure to companies like IBM and GE. Scott has been involved with companies in a wide variety of industries including direct marketing, retail, manufacturing, healthcare, and hospitality, just to name a few.

Scott has been recognized by the *Philadelphia Business Journal*, Philadelphia Chamber of Commerce and has been interviewed by the *Wall Street Journal* and featured in *Business Week*. He was part of the *Fast Company* events and has advised many companies that have grown into INC 500 winners. Scott is regarded as one of the regions foremost experts on entrepreneurship, venture capital, and succession planning. Scott is the go-to guy for many of the regions' private investment groups.

In addition to being an Optician, Scott attended the Wharton School of the University of Pennsylvania Entrepreneurial program. Scott serves on numerous boards and has served as Board Chair for the Philadelphia Workforce Development Corporation. He is also a speaker for SBA/ SCORE.

Scott has long played an active role in the Philadelphia area business community and is nationally known for his leadership in workforce development issues.

26757315R00067

Made in the USA
Charleston, SC
18 February 2014